Communication Styles Workbook

Tools for Discovering Your Personal Communication Style

Robert V. Keteyian

What's inside:

Introduction

In this workbook, you will make detailed observations about yourself and organize them into an understanding of your communication style. The exercises are designed to help you notice a broad range of experiences, from how you walk and talk to how you sleep and think. There are so many times we say, "Oh, that's just me," or "I guess I'm just a little weird." None of us have the opportunity to experience another's perceptions—we really are unique and literally experience the material world differently.

The sequence of activities begins with concrete observations about yourself and your interaction with others and guides you in using them to summarize your personal communication style, which is a blend of seven components:

1. **Interpersonal** (relating to others)
2. **Intrapersonal** (understanding self)
3. **Linguistic** (speaking)
4. **Logical** (reasoning)
5. **Visual-Spatial** (picturing)
6. **Kinesthetic** (experiencing/feeling)
7. **Auditory** (listening)

The activities that follow, if you do them all, will give you a comprehensive exploration of your communication style—its strengths and its weaknesses. This is a process that takes time. You may choose to do the activities systematically, or you may not. You may spend more time on some and skip others altogether—perhaps returning to them later. Some may simply not work for you. Take time to reflect, digest, and revisit as you progress. The activities are designed to be tools to help you define your style, a particular and personal style that accounts for your strengths, relative weaknesses, and quirks. Explore the workbook, and use the activities in the way that will best help you.

Personal Observation/Inventory

This Personal Observation/Inventory gives you an opportunity to scan your experience from top to bottom. You won't necessarily have specific observations in each area, but do start by going through it and making notes to reflect your initial reactions—the main ideas. From there, you may want to continue by noting what you observe about your behavior during the day.

In addition, you may want to ask someone you trust for input on areas that are hard to identify for yourself. Self-observation is, by its nature, very difficult. On the one hand, we know a lot about ourselves; on the other, it is very difficult to observe what is inherently natural and familiar.

Being self-conscious in this exercise does have its benefits. Logging what you eat or where and how you spend money is helpful when you want to lose weight or revise a household budget. This is no different. By noticing behavior and developing more awareness, it is much easier to make changes. Although our purpose here is not to promote change, developing more awareness is just as helpful in self-understanding.

This Personal Observation/Inventory is divided into five areas: physical, social, emotional, language, and creativity. The items listed under each are typical and provide an idea of the elements of the area. They are not intended to be absolute, so do add others that occur to you. As I stated earlier, some items will be easier than others to relate to. To avoid getting mired with an item you are uncertain about, let it go and return to it later. And if it never clicks for you, that won't affect your being able to define your communication style.

Physical	Things to Consider	How This Relates to Me
Gross Motor	walking style, activity level, fluidity of movement	
Fine Motor	dexterity, precision	
Energy	high/low, amount, consistency	
Relaxation	active/passive, regular pattern/spontaneous, indoor/outdoor	
Sleeping	amount, naps, night waking	
Dreams	frequency, vividness, recurring, enjoyment/fear, recall	
Eating	likes/dislikes, frequency, amount, relationship to energy, texture	

Vision	sensitivity to light, night vision, color appreciation, observant/nonobservant	
Touch	strong/gentle, comfort/ discomfort, sensitivity	
Smell	level of sensitivity, preferences	
Hearing	sensitivity to sound, appreciation of sounds, importance of music	
Voice	enunciation, loud/soft, fluctuation/monotone	
Animal Nature	which animal(s) are you most akin to	
Other		

Social

Peers	number/type of friends, frequency of contact, degree of intimacy	
Group Involvement	type of groups, roles in group, frequency of contact, energizing or draining	
Authority Figures	compliant, challenging, admiring	
Other		

Emotional

Range of Emotions	accessibility, comfort with emotions	
Boundaries	clarity, absorbency, act in/act out	
Mood	consistent/variable, pattern(s), predominant mood	
Stress	general level, coping skills, predominant emotion	
Temperature	warm/cool, open/closed	

go on ▷

Soothing	self-soothing (how?), contact with others	
Color	preferences, response to color	
Other		

Language

Expressive	verbal ability, nonverbal communication	
Receptive	listening skills, sensitivity to nonverbal cues	
Conversation	precision of language, give-and-take, enjoyment, functional/expository	
Other		

Creativity

Imagination	level of activity, vividness, use as tool	
Problem Solving	synthesizing, brainstorming, enjoyment of challenge	
Sense of Passion	what activates a sense of passion, strong/elusive	
Expression	writing, fine art, crafts, music, dance, computer, gardening, etc.	
Focus	process vs. product	
Solitude	amount required, role of contemplation, relationship to natural world	
Organization	attention to detail, ability to follow through	
Ceremony	family ceremonies, private rituals	
Other		

Communication Observations

This exercise is best done more than once. The purpose here is for you to make observations in the categories listed below while engaging in conversation with one or two others. What do you notice about yourself when you are talking with a friend, a child, a spouse, or a coworker? Do you use your hands a lot? Do you use analogies when you explain something? Are you a storyteller?

You can see why this exercise is best repeated. We communicate according to the relationship—formally and informally, for example—so it's good to have several opportunities to evaluate in trying to zero in on your strong characteristics and tendencies. Using a video camera might be useful as well. Most people who have done this are self-conscious initially but, after a few minutes, find their natural selves appear front and center. It can be fun (and sometimes a little embarrassing) to watch yourself, but I guarantee you will learn things about how you communicate.

Note that the chart includes sample observations. These are examples only. Your observations for any category may be slightly different.

Category	Examples	My Observations
Eye Contact	I make brief but frequent eye contact. I find eye contact distracting, and I lose track of the conversation.	
Physical Movements	I fidget a lot when I speak but am still when listening. I hardly move a muscle when I talk with someone.	
Gestures	I use gestures to explain or emphasize a point. I nod a lot.	
Facial Expressions	My face shows little affect. My face moves in harmony with the other person's expressions.	
Metaphors	Metaphors are the only way I can explain something. I never use metaphors. They confuse me.	

go on ▷

Sense of Sequence	I like to lay out everything in no particular order. Then I can discuss it. I need to arrange my thoughts in a specific order.	
Active Listening	I do a lot of reflecting back what I heard. I don't like to characterize or interrupt others.	
Quiet Listening	I often say uumm or uh-huh. I never know when to insert myself in the talk. I give others time to complete their thoughts.	
Care with Words	I work hard to use just the right word. I paint pictures with words. I pay more attention to getting the feeling.	
Rhythm and Cadence	I usually vary my tone of voice and/or talk really fast. I like to be very measured when speaking.	
Feeling Words	I use the word feeling frequently in conversation. I usually describe the situation, excluding the feelings at first.	
Visual References	I frequently say, "Oh, I see what you're saying." I often ask, "How does it look to you?"	
Auditory References	I often say "I hear what you're saying" or "It sounds like you are saying ___."	

Communication Component Inventory

After completing the Personal/Observation Inventory and gathering information from the Communication Observations exercise, it's time to use the Communication Component Inventory to help you develop a relationship to each component. The best way to approach this is to take a first pass through the items in each section—just go through them easily, casually, but seriously asking yourself, "Is this me?" or "Is this mostly true about me?" Skip any item you're uncertain about.

How you make notes doesn't matter. Writing *yes* or *no*, checking those that apply to you and leaving blank those that don't, and using colored markers with your own system of noting preferences or likenesses (i.e., red for the strongest preferences, blue for secondary strength, green for least in each section) are three possibilities. Other approaches include numbering the items under each component 1–5, strongest to least, and using personal symbols (i.e., stars and facial expressions). This is your inventory, so use a system that is most clear to you.

Keep in mind that the purpose of the inventory is to help you develop a relationship to each of the seven components and become increasingly familiar with your strengths and relative weaknesses. This is not a labeling exercise. In other words, you are not "an auditory person" or "a spatial person." You may, however, have a strong auditory component to your communication style that combines nicely with your interpersonal and linguistic components. These three elements may be the bedrock of your style that the other components rest on—and yes, they are all active simultaneously in every communication experience.

Interpersonal

_____ It's important for me to get my thoughts and feelings out in the open.
_____ I need to think out loud and discuss the same issue with several people.
_____ I enjoy re-visiting conversations with the same person.
_____ I prefer working with others on projects and goals.
_____ Others seek me out for counsel or advice.
_____ When I have a problem, talking things out is necessary and effective.
_____ I am good at drawing ideas together when working with others.
_____ I need a lot of feedback from others.
_____ I am intrigued by emotional dynamics in interpersonal relationships.

go on ▷

Intrapersonal

_____ I prefer to think things through before engaging in meaningful discussion.
_____ I need a lot of time to reflect and/or meditate.
_____ Learning about myself is central to my understanding of others.
_____ I have a clear understanding of my strengths and weaknesses.
_____ Explaining my inner process often seems irrelevant.
_____ To achieve clarity, I first need to be aware of my feelings, intentions, motivations, and goals.
_____ I plan thoughtfully and set goals for myself.
_____ My inner world naturally connects me to a universal perspective.
_____ I have a good sense of self-direction and think independently.

Linguistic

_____ I like to use words.
_____ I pay careful attention to the meaning of words.
_____ I often refer to something I've read when talking to others.
_____ Writing letters, stories, essays, etc., is an effective form of communication for me.
_____ I enjoy puns, plays on words, or other word games.
_____ I generally prefer reading a well written story to seeing it dramatized.
_____ I hear words in my head before speaking or writing them.
_____ I enjoy analyzing the use of language.
_____ I like explaining, teaching, or persuading others.

Logical

_____ I reason things through step-by-step when thinking and talking.
_____ I am intrigued by analyzing and problem solving.
_____ I prefer to follow a train of thought through to its logical conclusion without interruption.
_____ I like to find rational explanations for almost everything.
_____ I can think structurally in a way that cannot easily be translated into words.
_____ I can understand something if I can accurately quantify it.
_____ My understanding is often obscured by other people's feelings.
_____ I tend to look for patterns, relationships, and connections in understanding.
_____ I like to set up "what if . . ." experiments and play devil's advocate.

Visual-Spatial

_____ I easily perceive clear visual images when talking or listening.
_____ Meaning is never fixed—it moves and evolves over time.
_____ I remember things pictorially or symbolically.
_____ Color communicates a lot to me.
_____ I can see things from different angles when I hear a description.
_____ I can easily conceptualize the relationship between objects.
_____ Expressing in words the complexity of the visual images and relationships I perceive is difficult.
_____ I may seem spacey to others when I'm trying to explain something.
_____ I often use metaphor to explain something to others.

Kinesthetic

_____ Knowing registers as sensation in my body.
_____ Demonstrations really help me understand and express myself.
_____ I often fiddle with something or gesture while talking and listening.
_____ My sensory experience is very strong.
_____ I connect to others by demonstrating my feelings.
_____ Words alone are risky for me in communication.
_____ I need to physically experience things to understand them.
_____ I sense other's feelings and easily absorb their energy.
_____ Physical movement helps me process information.

Auditory

_____ I really notice tone of voice when someone is speaking.
_____ When I'm alone, I often hum, sing, or whistle.
_____ I can tell how someone feels by the sound of their voice.
_____ Music helps me think things through.
_____ I am acutely aware of everyday sounds, like the clink of a glass or the whoosh of a closing door.
_____ Familiar sounds, songs, jingles, etc. often stimulate my memory.
_____ Speaking out loud to myself helps bring greater clarity.
_____ I quietly repeat words and numbers to help me remember.
_____ I have a strong internal sense of rhythm.

Communication Components Summary

Now that you are farther down the path of self-observation, review the Communication Components table that follows. Take time to note your relationship to each component: Which ones resonate most strongly? Which may seem underdeveloped? Which do you primarily rely on? Do you seem balanced with all the components, or does only one really click?

Make notes relating to each component to summarize your experience. This might take the form of a poem for each (or some bullet points) or a numerical notation or color coding system. Don't shy away from being inventive and creative.

Component	Description	Notes
Interpersonal	Bouncing ideas off and brainstorming with others Thinking out loud Working for consensus	
Intrapersonal	Using time and space to clarify ideas and feeling Understanding one's self and experience as a vehicle for relating to others	
Linguistic	Meaning of words Conceptualizing linguistically Using descriptive language precisely	
Logical	Thinking sequentially (if A, then B, C, etc.) Following train of thought to logical conclusion without intrusion Quantifying to make sense of experiences	

Visual-Spatial	Using images	
	Seeing concepts three-dimensionally	
	Telling stories	
	Using metaphors to create understanding	
Kinesthetic	Feeling, sensing	
	Touching, smelling	
	Demonstrating	
Auditory	Tone of voice	
	Rhythm of speech	
	Timbre	
	Volume	

Style Activities

This is where you begin pulling together your observations and experiences from the previous activities to define your communication style. Have at hand the Personal/Observation Inventory, Communication Styles Inventory, Communication Observation, and Communication Components table. You will also need several sheets of paper (any size), a pen, and a pencil with an eraser. Markers or colored pencils are optional.

I suggest trying more than one of the following nine activities. One may be sufficient, but having different ways to approach understanding the relationship between the components is often helpful when defining your style.

Pie Chart

Draw a large circle, or use the circle with the examples below. Inside the circle, create seven pie-shaped wedges—three large, two medium, and two small. Now survey the inventories you filled out. Decide which three components stand out as your primary strengths, and write these names in the three largest wedges. Next, pick the two secondary components, and write those names in the medium-sized wedges. Fill in the two remaining components in the small sections.

Once you have completed this, take time to make the pie chart personal. For example, with the top three components try numbering them 1, 2, 3 to signify their relative importance. Repeat if you like with the other four areas. Be creative in making other notations, symbols, or colors to clarify your relationship to the components.

If you like, begin again with another pie chart or two and shift the size of the wedges to create different proportions and to more accurately reflect your developing awareness of your communication style. Remember, this is a process that will evolve as you clarify and refine your personal observations, understanding, and awareness. Repeat as many times as you find useful, or come back to it after you've tried some of the other activities.

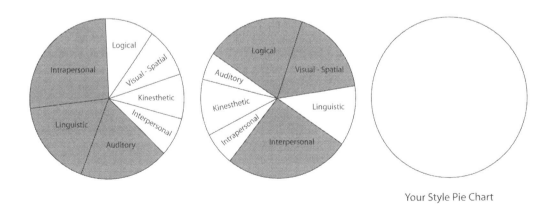

Your Style Pie Chart

Bar Graph

A bar graph is another way to look at the seven components in relation to each other. Follow the same format you used for the pie and create a bar graph or two or three to configure the components proportionally. (See the example below.)

When you find one that really seems to suit you, put it next to the pie chart that most reflects your style. Does either of these communicate the relationships of the components more clearly? Does one just feel right as a reflection of you? Don't worry if it still seems elusive. We'll be approaching this from other angles.

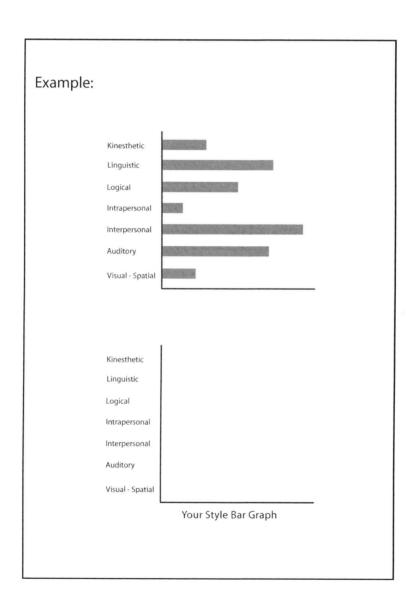

The Top Three

You've already selected the three communication components that are more dominant for you among the seven. Make notes about each of them, and then write about them. Create a brief paragraph (longer if you are linguistically inclined) describing how the component suits you or works in your life.

If you choose to be brief and to the point, list bullet-point notes for each component. Or consider writing an illustrative real-life anecdote or making up a story about each. You could, for example, approach it by associating each component to a different animal. In other words, use words in any way that best describes how you relate to these three (or seven if you wish) components. Be as spare or fanciful as you like.

Example 1:

The interpersonal component is the central organizing part of my style. The kinesthetic and linguistic components seem to funnel into and give strength to the interpersonal— and the auditory feels like a part of the linguistic. They are integral, although the linguistic often feels like the glue that holds it all together. I have to be conscious to include more of the intrapersonal. Though I tend to resist this, it is important in getting perspective and being more patient. The logical and visual-spatial seem like very distant cousins. I know they are there, and I do have a relationship to them, but they seem elusive.

Example 2:

The Interpersonal leads and has a strong place
The kinesthetic, linguistic/auditory complement the space.

Together they guide, give strength and ground
The interaction, feeling, words, and sound.

The Intrapersonal I sense and consciously include,
But the visual-spatial and logical mostly elude.

What Shape Is Your Style?

On another piece of paper, create various shapes that correlate to each component. For some of you, this won't make any sense at all; for others, it may be the most obvious thing to do. You'll need to experiment. Try something, and let it go if it doesn't work.

As you find shapes (or symbols) that fit the components (at least the top three), draw them in relation to each other on a separate piece of paper. Again, use color or other symbols for embellishment. Draw arrows or lines or squiggles between the shapes if it helps you connect and communicate something about the relationships between the components. Perhaps this will resemble more of a flow chart. Remember, this doesn't have to make sense to anyone else, and you don't have to explain it. The point is for it to work for you.

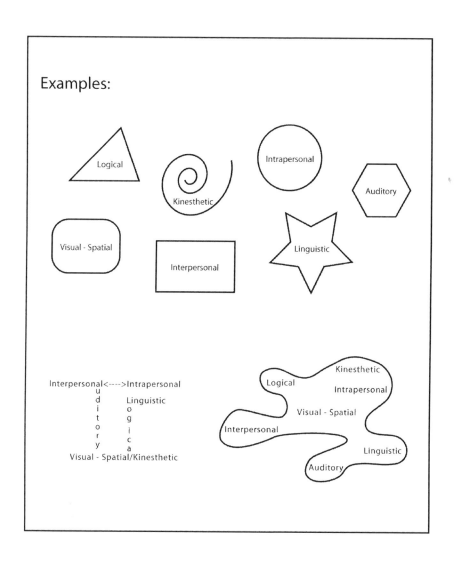

<u>Locate Your Style</u>

Draw a stick figure or rough outline of a human body, or use the blank figure on the next page. Sit quietly—perhaps with eyes closed—and relax for a few moments. After you relax, look directly at the human shape and begin imagining where you might locate each component in the body. For example, the linguistic might be in the mouth, but maybe it belongs in the heart or eyes. The interpersonal might be in the arms/hands or the ears if listening is the way you see yourself connecting to others. Please feel free to draw in other body parts: hair, more developed hands and feet, internal organs, etc.

This exercise requires some imagination, and it works well for some people but falls short for others. I suggest you give it a try even if you are reluctant or feel a little foolish, and if it doesn't work to better connect you to the communication components, then move on to another activity. Remember, this isn't a one-size-fits-all approach.

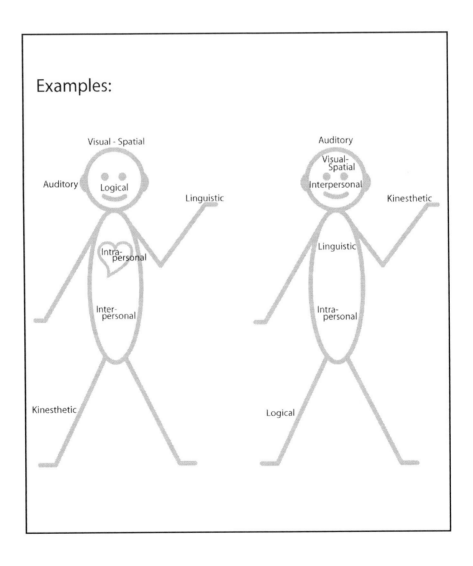

Locate Your Style

Components in Motion

A variation of the Locate Your Style activity is to actually move your own body to relate to each component. Again, begin by relaxing and getting quietly focused. Visualize the components in the body—that is, thinking of each or the top three—and feel where they belong in your body. From there, allowing your body to move naturally as an expression of the component helps establish a physical connection to it.

Working Together

If you process and learn better with a partner, then work with a partner to define your style. The educational concept of cooperative learning is ideal if you have a strong interpersonal component. Organize a study group of interested people—another individual or small group—and try each of the activities in this section of the workbook (or do the whole workbook). The give-and-take of interaction can stimulate your thinking, memories, and creativity. And it just might be more fun and interesting.

Workplace Evaluation

This activity helps by connecting the components to day-to-day life and offers a practical way to solve problems. Start by listing in the first column your duties at home or outside of home. In the second column, make note of what you like about this particular duty and, in the third column, what you don't like about it. For example, a teacher might list lunchroom duty. Perhaps she likes the informal contact with the kids as a way to better connect with them and dislikes the chaos and disciplinary actions required.

Duties	Like about it	Dislike about it	Communication components involved	Problem-solving ideas
lunchroom duty	informal contact	chaos and need for disciplinary action	positives: interpersonal linguistic negatives: auditory kinesthetic	storytelling or discussion groups, word games or activities

The fourth column gets to the heart of this activity. Which communication components are involved, relating to the likes and dislikes? In this situation, the teacher recognizes the importance of her interpersonal and linguistic components—connecting with and getting to know the kids better and sharing stories. This is the satisfying part of the duty for her. The dissatisfaction comes from the chaos (auditory and kinesthetic components) and conflicts that arise in an unstructured situation (all components!).

After identifying the communication components involved, the last step is to determine how to use your strengths to help deal with the negatives and/or problems that might arise. Specifically for our example, here are a few possibilities of how this teacher can capitalize on her interpersonal and linguistic strengths to mitigate the less desirable parts of lunchroom duty:

1. Hold informal storytelling groups. Provide a beginning story line and ask each student to add a line as they go around the table.
2. Start group discussions of recent sporting/news events, movie or TV programs.
3. Have partners or small groups brainstorm lists of rhyming words.
4. Give individuals, partners, or small groups number or sequence games to solve.
5. Have students use facial expressions and arms/hands to mime a sport, occupation, or other activity for other students at the table to figure out.

My Workplace Evaluation:

Duties	Like about it	Dislike about it	Communication components involved	Problem-solving ideas

Having completed one or more of the above activities, you have a pretty good idea of your communication strengths, relative weaknesses, and style. How could you represent the interplay graphically? For me, the interpersonal, kinesthetic, and auditory components form the foundation of my style, with the linguistic closely tied to the auditory as I experience them as integral (see diagram below). I rely most strongly on these components. The linguistic often feels like the glue that holds everything together. The spatial and logical I experience almost peripherally.

As you can see from my personal description, this is a highly subjective experience—no right and wrong. In fact, it has a fluidity that feels elusive. I emphasize this not to make it more complicated but because this is how it works.

Pay attention to the relationship you have with each of these components. You don't need to nail down a hierarchy, although if that works and is useful, then fine; but do take care not to be definitive if that boxes you in too much.

Bob Keteyian's Communication Style:

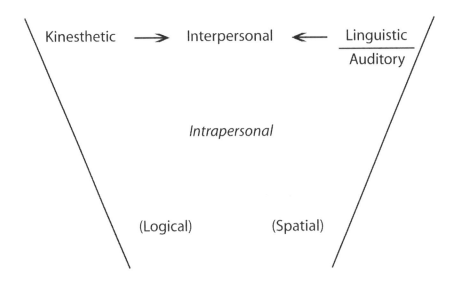

Now it is your turn to find a way to represent your own style, for your own use. Does it take the form of a written description, poem, bullet points? Is it something you can quantify with a formula or pie chart? Is it associated with movement—a dance, a piece of music, or a quiet meditation? Can you symbolize it in some graphic way or in the internal spatial domain? Perhaps it is just something you feel (have a feel for). Use the workspace below to plan, sketch, or execute a style depiction for yourself. Find your own way—this is your style after all, and it is clearly unique. It can evolve and change over time with your growing awareness, and it remains a tool to guide you in having more connected, successful communication with yourself and others.

Your style:

Proactive Problem Solving

Having organized the components of your communication style and recognized how they guide your communication, it is time to look at the shadow side. Our personal strengths have the potential to get us into trouble, and we can assume others are processing information the same way we do.

From the communication styles perspective, it is essential to recognize how your strengths can create potential problems. The communication guide that follows will help you zero in on your own challenging areas. It is organized into three columns: the first lists the components, the second summarizes the positive elements for each, and the third highlights the most common problems associated with each.

List your three most-developed components (or all of them if you like). For each component, review the potential problems associated in column 3. Make notes regarding the problems you can identify with.

Sometimes it helps to remember a recent conflict you have had with another person. By analyzing the interaction and using the potential problems column as a guide, you may be better able to identify how your style got you into trouble.

Try to identify a repetitive pattern of conflict you have had in a close relationship too. See if you can write out the sequence of conversation as a way to immerse yourself in the familiar pattern. Notice what words you use, how you feel, what your expectations and assumptions are. Try to remember your body language. Also, think about and try to remember what you heard, saw, and felt about the other person in the conflict.

This is probably the most challenging part of the workbook. It can be hard to observe your own behavior, analyzing the components and concomitant problems. If you can't remember a recent conflict or repetitive pattern of conflict in a close relationship, give yourself some time. By observing your strengths over time, you'll eventually get a better feel for the shadow side, especially if you make notes about your behavior.

Component	Elements	Potential Problems	My Problems
Interpersonal	in-depth conversation sounding board to think out loud continuity, achieving understanding over time	high frustration without enough feedback some things said are not meant expecting too much involvement from others	

go on ▷

Intrapersonal	time and space for self clarity of intentions, needs, and feelings choices, not directives	hard to give immediate feedback absorbed by own process overwhelmed by too many possibilities	
Linguistic	words, stories, letters defining terms developing concepts through words	invalidating nonverbal reality too fixed on defining words and concepts (losing essence of meaning) not giving others an opportunity to contribute to a conversation	
Logical	logical progression of ideas validating importance of sequence clear definition of problems and goals	discounting emotional process by focusing too much on content derailed by feedback in the middle of sequential process not enough inter-action (too much monologue)	
Visual-Spatial	describe or present a picture, image, or metaphor enough time to describe (unfold) the image or picture interrelatedness of parts to whole	uncomfortable translating pictures or images into words too diffuse or impressionistic (appears spacey) difficulty defining boundaries	

go on ▷

Kinesthetic	experiential involvement visceral response engaging the body (e.g., gestures)	hard to relate without experiencing feelings can obscure content can become overwhelmed by absorbing another's energy	
Auditory	how it sounds influences receptivity importance of rhythm, tone, and volume use of music to convey idea or feeling	infer wrong intent from tone of voice not taking content at face value	

Tools for Communication and Self-Understanding

As you become more natural working with your communication style, you will become aware of your less developed components as well. When you review the Tools for Communication and Self-Understanding table that follows, take time to survey each category. Start by circling any tool that especially suits you. Next, note those tools that you would like to explore, regardless of whether or not it is associated with one of your strengths. You want to expand your communication repertoire, not limit yourself.

Perhaps you are not strong in the auditory component. Then make an effort to involve yourself in some listening activities, paying careful attention to how you listen or don't listen. See what you can learn. You may discover that by being more aware and intentional, you can employ some of the less developed components better than you imagined.

It is hard to categorize some of the tools. Listening to audio recordings, for example, could be part of the linguistic or the auditory. Don't be concerned about the specific categorization; think more about what works for you and how you would like to develop your communication skills.

Once you've explored this table and zeroed in on the tools that interest you the most and on those you wish to learn more about, we'll wrap up.

Component	Need	Tools	Notes
Interpersonal	Interaction	theater/psychodrama, simulations, selective self-disclosure, feedback, leadership roles, support group, group therapy, active listening, modeling, intuition	
Intrapersonal	Going Within	journal, choices (*Would it be better to ___ or ___?*), dreams, solitude (*Think of a time when ___. What kind of space do you need for ___.*), explore core human conditions, meditation, retreats, identity quest	
Linguistic	Words	carefully defined concepts, writing (journal, letters, essays), self-help reading, listening to tapes, poetry, humor, interpretations, questions, teaching	

go on ▷

Logical	Reasoning	personality assessments, quantify experience/events (numbers, graphs, etc.), sequences, experiments, question/hypothesis or problem-solving formats, logical consequences, genograms, contracts	
Visual-Spatial	Picture/Metaphor	guided imagery, naturally occurring images, dream work, symbols, graphs, genograms, drawing, art therapy, color, stories, free association, doodling, mind mapping	
Kinesthetic	Somatic Sensation	drama, relaxation training, family sculpting, movement exercises, objects of meaning (e.g., stone, picture), focus on body, videotape, vision quest, yoga, massage therapy, acupuncture, dance, martial arts	
Auditory	Rhythmic/Melodic Sense	audiotapes, use of music, biofeedback with tones, tone of voice, pitch, music therapy, free association, reframing, sounds from natural world, rhythmic movement	

Your Communication Style

Now it's time to synthesize your ideas and observations from the previous activities and map your communication style. Start by listing the communication components in order of their importance to you. For example:

1. Interpersonal
2. Kinesthetic
3. Auditory
4. Linguistic

5. Intrapersonal
6. Visual-Spatial
7. Logical

Begin a two-column chart. In the first column, list, symbolize, or otherwise depict the top three or four components. In the second column, list the tools that are best suited to you for each component. For example:

Component	Tools
Interpersonal	Need/give feedback, intuition, active listening, modeling
Kinesthetic	Relaxation training, exercise, videotaping

Now make a three-column chart—there's a blank one to use on the next page. Again, list the top components in the first column. In the second column, note the potential problems you have identified; and in the third column, brainstorm ideas to avoid the potential problems. For example:

Component	Potential Problems	Remedies
Interpersonal	a. say things that aren't meant b. expect too much	a. tell others "thinking out loud" b. take responsibility for your own needs
Kinesthetic	a. feeling obscures content b. absorb too much energy	a. make sure I balance content and feeling when listening b. maintain personal limits

go on ▷

Component	Potential Problems	Remedies

Notes:

Summarizing Your Style

The example in your three-column chart is one way of pulling together an understanding of your style. It is straightforward, but you might want to organize the pieces in a more personal way—for example, by making a video or audio recording, drawing or symbolizing the information, writing a story, or creating a movement activity. Your depiction should best account for your style. Such a summary to use as a quick reference is good to have. It helps reinforce new learning and reminds you of particular details that are easy to overlook. This is a new framework for you, and it takes time to take it in. Make sure you refer to it regularly so it becomes embedded in your awareness.

Be sure to refer to your summary when things aren't going well—you've just had a fight with your partner, child, or coworker; or perhaps you've been out of sorts and not feeling very focused. By getting better connected to your style, you automatically focus on your strengths, which is a much better basis for problem solving and addressing conflict resolution.

Finally, it is useful to evaluate your style summary from time to time because we do change. As you work with this paradigm, you will gain new insights and understanding. There might be nuances in your style that you were previously unaware of, or perhaps because you decided to put more attention on a lesser-developed component, it has a stronger place in your concept of style.

Remember, all these components are active concurrently and are synchronistic. I've broken them down to foster an understanding of the parts; they actually do function as a whole. Your style is part of you. It is not you. It is not who you are, but it says a lot about how you operate. It is another lens through which you can see yourself and how you interact with others and solve problems. I refer to it as a practical tool with very broad application, compatible with virtually any theory of personality or change.

Robert Keteyian is an interpersonal communication consultant and licensed counselor, offering workshops and training for both individuals and groups. With a master's degree in Counseling Psychology, he focuses on promoting and developing good communication practices in families and in the workplace. He is the author of *Do You Know What I Mean?—Discovering Your Personal Communication Style.*

For more information or to contact Bob regarding consultation services, speaking engagements, workshops, and communication styles training, visit **www.communicationstyles.us**. Also at the website is Bob's blog, "Thinking Out Loud," where he posts on a variety of communication topics and issues.

9084329R0